HOW TO LIVE WITH AN UNBELIEVER

Jo Berry

PYRANEE
BOOKS

Zondervan Publishing House
Grand Rapids, Michigan

How to Live With an Unbeliever

This book is excerpted from *Beloved Unbeliever*, copyright © 1981 by Jo Berry.

This is a Pyranee Book
Published by the Zondervan Publishing House,
1415 Lake Drive, S.E., Grand Rapids, Michigan 49506

Library of Congress Cataloging in Publication Data

Berry, Jo
    How to live with an unbeliever.

    "Excerpted from Beloved unbeliever. c1981"—Cip t.p. verso.
    "Pyranee book"—CIP t.p. verso.
    1. Wives—Religious life. 2. Marriage—Religious aspects—Christianity. 3. Witness bearing (Christianity) I. Berry, Jo. Beloved unbeliever. II. Title.
BV4527.B48 1986   248.8'435   86-18983
ISBN 0-310-42622-7

Printed in the United States of America

86 87 88 89 90 / 10 9 8 7 6 5 4 3 2

Contents

1

Being a Suitable Helper

It appears that one of the biggest problems an unequally yoked wife faces is that she believes she is different from other Christian wives. She is hurtfully aware of how many church activities are planned for couples. She's the one whose husband won't come with her to the Wednesday night potluck, the Christmas cantata, or the Sunday school program. She can't pray or read the Bible with him. She sees herself as an exception, rather than a rule, so dwells on how different her marriage is.

Perhaps those of us who are married in the faith perpetuate this myth; somehow we mirror the idea that every event in our lives, from mopping floors to buying a new car, happens on some sort of super-spiritual level, when in reality Christian couples also have differences. They fight. They don't always believe alike or agree on how to raise the kids, how much money to give to the church, or where to go on vacation.

Christian husbands come home from work tired and frustrated. They lose their tempers. They yell at the kids. They don't always pray with their wives when they are distressed, nor do they conduct nightly devotions with wisdom and wit. Christian husbands and wives are just as human, and sometimes as carnal, as unbelievers are.

As a result of this misconception, the unequally yoked wife tends to "idealize" Christian marriage and possibly blame many normal marriage problems on the fact that her husband is an unbeliever. She is positive that if her husband

1

came to Christ her marriage would be blissful and almost problem free. Each of the women I interviewed for this book said that although she intellectually knows all marriages have pitfalls and problems, she has (or had) the unrealistic expectation that if her husband would accept Christ, her marriage would become one of the "made in heaven" variety.

Because an unequally yoked marriage lacks the spiritual quality that Christian marriages have, she may even become jealous of her sisters who are married to believers. She may silently play a game called, "If only he was a Christian," which makes it more difficult for her to be a good wife or to be satisfied and enjoy her marriage.

Tammy explained her feelings this way: "I have always idealized thoughts of a Christian marriage, to the point where I was envious of women who are married to believers. I have realized this is wrong. One day I thought, what if God said, 'Tammy, Rod is never going to commit his life to Me. Now, what are you going to do about your marriage?' "

She continued, "One thing is sure, I couldn't sit around waiting for him to be saved. God showed me that our happiness cannot depend on whether he comes to Christ. Facing that made me look at myself and see that I was not the wife God wanted me to be. Now, I am freer. It is easier to enjoy being with Rod because I don't think of him as my unsaved husband but as the man I love, with whom I will spend the rest of my natural life. What happens in eternity is in God's hands."

Tammy has learned what each unequally yoked wife must: that in God's eyes a wife is a wife is a wife, regardless of the status of her husband. The Lord has assigned specific roles and duties for all wives, whether they are married to believers or unbelievers. If an unequally yoked wife understands her role and what God expects from her, she can minister to her husband more effectively and have a transforming impact on his life.

What it Means to be a Helpmeet (Helper)

Basically, God wants an unequally yoked wife to be what He wants any Christian wife to be—a godly, loving companion to her husband. Physically, the Lord created man before He created woman. He fellowshiped with Adam in the Garden and gave him work to do. But the Lord God knew He had one more thing to do before Paradise was complete. He said, "It is not good for the man to be alone; I will make him a helper suitable for him" (Gen. 2:18), thereby establishing a wife's primary role: that of being a helpmeet to her husband.

The word "helpmeet" or "helper" contains many subtle meanings. A key meaning is the idea of suitability. The Amplified Bible reads, "I will make him a helper meet (suitable, adapted, completing) for him." A wife is fashioned by God, both in her physical and emotional make-up, to be complementary to her husband: to adapt to and complete him.

She is the balancing component in his life. Where he is weak, she is strong; where he lacks sensitivity, she is tender; where he is vulnerable, she is firm. And because a husband/wife team is structured to enhance each other's good points and supplement each other in areas of weakness, a wife can be her husband's greatest asset and aid. She can be used by God in unique, exciting, creative ways because she is suited to help him.

The word "helper" is the same word that is used elsewhere in Scripture to illustrate that God is our helper—our strength, guide, and undergirder. This is not a passive position but a vital, active, dynamic one. And just as Eve was created for Adam, to fulfill and complete his life, each wife was chosen and ordained by God for her particular husband. She is suitable for him, so she can have a special ministry to him and contribute to his life in ways that no one else can. She was made to assist and accompany him. The Lord

3

will use her to nurture her husband intellectually, emotionally, and spiritually, if she is willing.

Simply put, a wife is to be the same kind of helper to her husband that God is to His bride, the church! This dynamic duty embodies several elements. One is the idea of protection. God is "our help and our shield" (Ps. 33:20), so as a helpmeet, a wife is responsible for assisting and shielding her husband.

This runs contrary to our cultural concept of the man protecting the woman, doesn't it? Yet, any wife knows that there are many ways in which she shields her husband. She may guard him from unnecessary problems, set a peaceful atmosphere in the home, and do whatever she can to alleviate stress in his life. She protects his health by cooking the right kinds of foods and should be concerned for both his physical and spiritual well-being. At times, when appropriate, she will shelter him from situations that will hurt him. She takes care of him and ministers to his needs by doing things for him that will make his life easier.

A Good Helpmeet is Faithful

Ministering in this capacity also involves a foundational element called trust. God, our role model, is a faithful helper. Scripture proclaims, "Great is Thy faithfulness" (Lam. 3:23). The Lord isn't just a little bit trustworthy. His faithfulness is expansive, deep, immense, overwhelming! He never lets us down. He is always there when we need Him, so much so that He acts on our behalf even when we are not aware He is intervening. A wife who is a true helpmeet will be there for her husband in the same way. He will know he can always, under any circumstances, depend on her.

A godly wife will manifest the kind of fidelity that allows "the heart of her husband [to trust] in her" (Prov. 31:11). Her husband will know he can rely on her with his total being, certain that, "She [will do] him good and not evil all the days of her life" (Prov. 31:12).

4

A wife who emulates God in her role as helper has a faith that endures; a total, permanent commitment to her husband that lasts throughout the marriage. She "bears all things, believes all things, hopes all things, endures all things" (1 Cor. 13:7).

A Good Helpmeet is a Counselor

Another component of being a suitable helper is that of counselor; being a sounding board and a resource person of inestimable value. This is an area where many Christian wives experience confusion. They mistakenly believe that it is not submissive to give advice to their husbands, to share ideas and opinions, to make suggestions, or to differ with them. God is our counselor. David noted, "With Thy counsel Thou wilt guide me" (Ps. 73:24). Likewise, God uses a wife's counsel to guide her husband.

In a marriage, where two are one flesh, what one partner does affects the other. It is especially important in an unequally yoked marriage, where the unbeliever does not have any other source for the counsel of the Lord except his wife, that she incorporate scriptural ideals and principles into their lifestyle by the advice she offers and the values she maintains.

When Winifred and I met for coffee, she was so frustrated she was on the verge of tears. "Sam wants to take all the money we've saved for the down payment on a house and buy a boat, a stupid twelve thousand dollar boat!" Obviously, she was angry. I knew she had kept her job and delayed having children so they could save the cash for a home. No wonder she was upset.

I asked the inevitable question: "What was Sam's reaction when he saw how upset you are and when you told him you wouldn't go along with buying a boat with the house money?"

She dabbed at her eyes with a tissue and said, "I didn't say anything." She went on to explain that she was afraid to say something, for fear she would be breaking God's command to "be submissive to your own husbands so that even if any of them are disobedient to the word, they may be won without a word by the behavior of their wives" (1 Peter 3:1).

We spent the next one-and-one-half hours talking about the balance between submission and passivity. When she left she was confident she could make her husband see how foolish it would be to buy the boat, in light of the long range effect it would have on their lives. They wanted a home and children, and Winifred wasn't willing to sacrifice those for a water sport.

She called later to tell me that Sam had been quite reasonable once she started communicating with him. But what if she hadn't performed her role as counselor? She'd be nursing anger, bitterness, and resentment. And they wouldn't be the proud owners of a new house. Mainly, she would have done them both a disservice by not speaking out.

Unequally yoked wives tell me they frequently feel they don't have much influence over their husbands; that what they say and think doesn't matter. I don't believe that. I think the problem is that they do not know how to communicate. They are afraid they'll leave their Christianity open to criticism if they take a firm stand or advise their husbands. Open, honest communication is essential to any marriage, regardless of the spiritual standing of either party. Instead of forsaking her position as counselor, the unequally yoked wife needs to learn how to properly communicate her ideas and to be such a wise and loving resource person that her husband will come to rely on her advice and opinions.

A Good Helpmeet is a Companion

Along with helpmeet, another wifely role mentioned in Genesis 2:18 (LB) is that of companion.

God noted that it is not good for man to be alone. He

6

wanted man to understand that too, so He did an interesting thing. After He determined He would "make a helper suitable for him" (Gen. 2:18), He didn't immediately make woman. Instead, He made the lower animals and birds, then brought them to Adam so he could name them. And after Adam had named all of the beasts of the field and birds of the sky, he realized that among all those creatures there wasn't one that was suitable to be his companion; one who was complementary to him, with whom he could have fellowship.

I think the Lord God chose that way to show man that he is incomplete without woman; that no other living creature can fulfill his needs the way she can. Adam needed a wife—a companion and friend—so he would not be lonely, but would have someone with whom to share his life.

The unequally yoked wife must be careful not to neglect this aspect of her marriage relationship. Many have told me that they would rather talk to and be with their Christian friends than with their husbands, because those friends understand things their husbands can't. While that may be true, there are many non-spiritual things wives can share with their husbands.

Rene and Andy have been married for thirty-two years. They golf together, play tennis, go to the theater and ballet. They travel a lot. They have a wide circle of friends and generally enjoy each other and their life together. They are what I would call a close, loving couple.

Rene is a Christian and Andy is not. She accepted the Lord when they had been married eight years. When I asked her how she had managed to gain such a balance in her life, she told me she decided that the only thing she and her husband did not have in common was Christ, but that she was going to share every other area of her life with him.

"I loved him when I married him. His zest for life and his diverse interests were what attracted me to him in the first place. I don't think God wants to interfere with our

7

relationship, but make it better. And, He has." Rene is a lady who knows how to be a friend and companion to her husband.

Solomon, in describing what a friend is, said he or she is someone who "loves at all times" (Prov. 17:17) and "sticks closer than a brother" (Prov. 18:24). Jesus noted that the ultimate act of friendship is a willingness to sacrifice self. "Greater love has no one than this, that one lay down his life for his friends" (John 15:13). Part of a wife's role is to be that kind of friend to the man she married.

A Good Helpmeet is a Willing Sexual Partner

Beyond companionship, a wife is to be a willing sexual partner for her husband. This part of the relationship is not to be maintained out of duty or obligation, but out of love and desire. God told Eve, "You shall bring forth children; yet your desire shall be for your husband" (Gen. 3:16). It is normal for a wife to want a physical relationship with her husband. This is true whether or not he is a believer.

Several years ago, when I was taping a Bible course called, "Sex Within Marriage: God's View," I asked the women to submit their questions in writing. One of the most pertinent was turned in by an unequally yoked wife who said, "I'm married to an unbeliever. Neither of us were Christians when we were married. I came to Christ and my husband hasn't. Although I love him very much, I feel guilty every time we have intercourse because I'm plagued by the idea that I'm joining a child of Satan with a child of God. This has really decreased my enjoyment. What should I do?"

I'm sure that other women in her position may feel the same way. A look into God's Word should alleviate their anxiety. First, we find that God thought up the idea of sex: "male and female He created them" (Gen. 1:27). Then He divinely and sovereignly instituted marriage. He physically formed woman from the man, then had them unite in a one-

8

flesh relationship. Sexual intercourse sealed the marriage commitment. And it must have been a natural act because "the man and his wife were both naked and were not ashamed" (Gen. 2:25). So not only is sex God-created but it is God-ordained within a marriage.

The apostle Paul taught, while dealing specifically with the unequally yoked situation, that God does not view sexual intercourse between a Christian and his or her unbelieving mate as joining a child of God with a child of Satan. Instead, in His grace He sees it as sanctified—pure and holy—because one of His children is involved.

When a Christian woman is married to an unbeliever, that marriage is looked upon by God as set apart and separate from the world. In His eyes, the union with an unbeliever is still godly and holy. The marriage is clothed in Christ's righteousness because the believer is. The marriage is sanctified and the husband lives in the presence of the Holy Spirit, who is at work in the life of the believing wife. Because of this, the unequally yoked wife is completely free to enjoy a full, meaningful sexual relationship with her husband. She can rest on the promise that God looks upon their children with favor and blessing. "The unbelieving husband is sanctified through his wife . . . for otherwise your children are unclean, but now they are holy" (1 Cor. 7:14).

A Good Helpmeet Makes Him Proud

Within the basic role of helper and of being a friend and lover to her husband, a wife is faced with multitudes of responsibilities. One is that she will please her husband. Proverbs 12:4 observes, "An excellent wife is the crown of her husband, but she who shames him is as rottenness in his bones."

A wife is always on display as part of her husband's identity. She is "Mrs." He "wears" her as a ruler would a crown. She is an obvious, noticeable, highly visible part of

9

his life. And every man wants to be able to point to his wife with pride.

Unbelieving husbands, however, tell me that they are sometimes ashamed of their Christian wives because they are so critical, if not in words than in attitude, of everything they do, of their friends, and of the places they go. They are embarrassed by their wives' "religion," and as difficult as it may be to accept, that is a legitimate complaint. Unbelieving husbands are afraid their wives will come off as fanatics, as "holier than thou," to people they care about.

One man told me his wife was always outwardly pleasant to his friends. Although she didn't talk to them much, she was cordial. But, he said, "When we're working on the car or playing cards, and she brings us sandwiches and beer, she slams them onto the table or acts as if her hands are dirty because she touched a beer bottle." This embarrasses him, but when he tried to explain to his wife how her attitude was coming across, she (in his words) "lectured me on the evils of drinking." And he couldn't understand why she had to make such a big deal about a couple of drinks.

He found a way to solve the problem. He and his friends just go somewhere else because, "I don't feel welcome in my own home when I'm doing certain things my wife disapproves of."

A wife, any wife, is to be a crown to her husband, and if an unequally yoked wife makes major issues out of minor ones, she will drive her husband from her *and* from the Lord. Regardless of her own standards, she must be extremely careful not to embarrass him or put him down. She needs to remember that Christ, who is her example, was always right out there among the drinkers, gluttons, prostitutes, and sinners. That was how He reached them with His love. She has to learn how to show her disapproval without being condemning or judgmental. She must try to be such a great wife that her unbelieving husband can point to her as "an excellent wife."

A Good Helpmeet Does Things God's Way

She won't be able to do this if her attitude is not right; if she is silently critical or acts as if she is "better" than her unsaved husband and his associates. It's a fact of life that we convey our feelings through our actions more than by what we say. So the unequally yoked wife must exercise special care not to play the martyr; not to come across as if her marriage is a cross she has to bear for the Lord's sake. Any negative attitudes will show, so she needs to cultivate positive, godly thoughts that will shine from her countenance.

Frequently we look at the virtuous woman in Proverbs 31 from the standpoint of her performance, but the more I read and dwell on that passage, the more I am struck by her attitude. She's a nice person who enjoys life and is fun to be around. For instance, she's a cheerful doer. "She works with her hands in delight" (Prov. 31:13).

This excellent wife in Proverbs 31 is also excited about being a wife. She's industrious and energetic and does everything wholeheartedly. But the thing that stands out the most about her is that she has a pleasant disposition. "She opens her mouth in wisdom, and the teaching of kindness is on her tongue" (Prov. 31:26). She isn't so distracted by what she's doing that she yells at the kids and nags her husband. She is happy and content. "She senses that her gain is good; and she smiles at the future" (Prov. 31:18, 25).

She doesn't go around talking about what a godly woman she is. She *lives* her faith and lets "her works praise her in the gates" (Prov. 31:31). And her husband is her biggest fan! He praises her publicly when he sits with the elders in the city gates. He thinks she's the best wife who ever lived, and he tells her so. "Many daughters have done nobly, but you excel them all" (Prov. 31:29). What wife wouldn't want to hear those words?

Interestingly, we are not told anything about her husband's faith or his spiritual status. But we see that because she was the kind of woman God wanted her to be, she had a happy home and a contented, loving husband.

Our homes are where we live. An unequally yoked wife can have immeasurable influence there. If she is wise, she will take advantage of her domestic setting and use it as a womb in which the Lord can woo and win her husband into birth in God's kingdom. She can use their home and her God-given position as a wife to counterbalance the worldliness that predominates her husband's life. She must be open to the wonder of their love. She must devote herself to him, the same as she would if he were the greatest Christian who ever lived.

She needs to learn to separate her personal reactions to what her husband does from the actual agitation of the Holy Spirit. And above all, she must do everything within her power to be the kind of helper, friend, and counselor to her unbelieving husband that God meant her to be.

2

Being a First-Peter-Three Partner

Although being a helpmeet is a wife's primary responsibility, there are many variances in the way that role is implemented. The situation of an unequally yoked wife differs from that of women who are married to Christians. So God has given her a basic principle of action which, if adhered to, enables her to be used as a constructive instrument in her husband's life.

That principle is found in 1 Peter 3:1-4. "You wives, be submissive to your own husbands so that even if any of them are disobedient to the word, they may be won *without a word* by the behavior of their wives, as they observe your chaste and respectful behavior. And let not your adornment be external only—braiding the hair and wearing gold jewelry, and putting on dresses; but let it be the hidden person of the heart, with the imperishable quality of a gentle and quiet spirit, which is precious in the sight of God."

In His grace, the Lord lovingly gave those instructions. While there is no panacea, no simple solution to the multitude of dilemmas these unequally yoked women face, it includes a positive plan of action.

It offers the hope that if a Christian wife is obedient, she may win her husband to the Lord through the example of her godly behavior. It tells her how to be a First-Peter-Three Partner.

While this imposition of silence is difficult, St. Gregory wisely observed, "It is needful that we sometimes endure,

13

keeping to ourselves what evil men are, in order that they may learn in us, by our good living, what they are not." That is a perfect description of the responsibility of the unequally yoked wife.

God's formula contains a positive approach to the marriage—be submissive—and wields some common sense advice on what not to do: Do not try to talk an unsaved husband to the Lord. God has good reasons for imposing such a stringent restriction. One is that it is so easy to say one thing and be another. If a wife tries to "preach" her husband to Christ while she is failing by example, she will only alienate him further.

Also, if she tries to point out his sin to him, she will create unbearable friction in their marriage. All unsaved people hate to be told about their sin. It causes a terrible dilemma for them. If they deny it, they look foolish, because sin is so obvious. If they admit it, they also are admitting they need to be saved from it, or that they should take steps to correct what they are doing. Saying, "I am a sinner," is the first overture of repentance that leads to the cross.

So, if a woman verbally accuses her husband of his sin, she puts him in an impossible situation. She will cause dissension in her home. And, chances are her husband will not listen to her, but will retaliate with a few instances of her imperfections which he would like to see eliminated.

Also, verbalizing won't work because it is impossible to communicate spiritual truth to an unspiritual person. It is like trying to carry on a conversation with a baby who is still in the womb, who hasn't yet been born. That infant can't relate to what is said nor understand the content of the message. The same is true with a person who has not been born spiritually. Nagging, lecturing, or explaining will not bring a person to the Lord, because "the natural, nonspiritual man does not accept or welcome or admit into his heart the gifts and teachings and revelations of the Spirit of God, for they are folly (meaningless nonsense) to him; and he is *incapable* of knowing them" (1 Cor. 2:14 Amplified).

The unequally yoked wife must understand this, not just with her intellect, but with her heart. *Nothing she says about God will make her husband love the Lord or want to turn his life over to Him.* Regeneration is an act of the Holy Spirit. God uses people to bring about that process, but only if they do what He has instructed. He has told women who are unequally yoked not to try to communicate verbally about spiritual things with their unbelieving mates. The problem in following this principle is in deciding how to practice it so one can be used as God's silent instrument of salvation.

Marriage is a Partnership

If a Christian wife is effectively to act out this principle, she needs to grasp the full meaning of what marriage is, and what submission is and is not. Too many unequally yoked wives place an unfair burden on themselves because they do not understand that their marriages are no different from all other marriages except in the way they are to handle spiritual matters. Marriage is a partnership, regardless of the spiritual state of either person. But in an unequal matching, the believing wife must separate the spiritual from the secular aspects of the relationship.

The Lord has commanded that she *not* communicate with her husband. This means she is not to communicate about the things of God. In all other matters, she is free, as a marriage partner, to share her feelings and opinions and to advise her husband.

She must not confuse cultural standards with biblical ones. Lifestyle issues—such as who changes diapers, who mows the lawn, who mops the floor, should a wife be employed outside of her home, decisions about how money is spent, what color to paint the walls, and where to go on vacation—are not spiritual issues. These kinds of things

15

should be decided by each couple, based on what they believe is best for their marriage, within the framework of their own personalities and family structure.

Yet, many unequally yoked wives I interviewed told me they always give in to their unbelieving husbands, even in secular matters where they disagree, because they do not want to be non-submissive. In actuality, by withholding vital communication they are failing in their role as helper, counselor, and companion.

Of course, there will be times when a delicate balance exists between submission and non-submission, so it is imperative that the unequally yoked wife fathom what submission is and what it is not, so she can draw the necessary distinctions between when to give in and when to stand her ground.

What Submission is And is Not

Most importantly, she must understand that submission is not blind obedience, although obedience is sometimes a by-product of submission. Whereas obedience is following orders, submission is voluntarily surrendering or yielding the will. In Scripture, wives are exhorted to submit or subject themselves to their husbands. Children are told to obey. (See Col. 3:18, 20 and Eph. 5:22; 6:1.) And there is a vast difference between the role of a wife and that of a child. Obedience doesn't leave room for choice; submission does.

Phyllis is a woman who, in her desire to please the Lord and win her husband, almost ruined her marriage because she didn't comprehend the difference between obedience and submission. She and Dan had been married over six years when she accepted Christ. She is an outgoing, fun-loving, spunky person and Dan loves her wit and her independent spirit. She told me that he is always telling her one of the things he appreciates most about her is that she is a capable, self-sufficient person, "and that he can't stand women who are clinging vines."

16

Immediately after Phyllis came to the Lord she started attending a women's Bible study. The topic was submission, and somehow she got a limited perspective about it. She wanted to have a gentle and quiet spirit, so she stopped discussing things with Dan, the way she had prior to her conversion, and didn't clown around as much. No matter what he suggested, she smiled and agreed. She was miserable, because she was squelching her personality, and Dan was "on her case" all the time, asking if she was mad at him or not feeling well.

Finally, one night, just to see if he could get a normal reaction from her, he told her that he'd been offered a transfer and that they were going to move to Alaska. Submissive wife that she'd become, she gulped back tears, seethed inside and nodded. Dan blew! He accused her of not loving him any more and not caring what happened in their lives. He screamed that she had changed so much it was like living with a stranger. Phyllis burst into tears and tried to explain that she was just trying to be a good wife. Her husband's reply was, "Well, if this is what God does for you, who wants Him?"

The next day she went to her pastor for counsel and he was able to clarify her misconceptions. He invited her and Dan to go with him and his family to a baseball game. He made Phyllis promise not to mention the Lord all evening, to enjoy the game the way she always did.

That was three years ago. Dan still hasn't accepted Christ, but he sometimes goes to church with Phyllis and is open to being friends with Christians. And she has returned to her outgoing, sparkling self. She learned the hard way that submission and obedience are not synonymous.

Submission is for all Christians

Another misjudgment is that submission is "for women only." It is not. Submission is an attitude of a Christ-centered life. It is humility in practice; compliance to the leading of the Holy Spirit. The Bible teaches that children are to submit to parents, citizens to government, young men and Christians to their leaders, and ultimately, we are all to "be subject to one another in the fear of Christ" (Eph. 5:21).

All of us in the family of God are to, "do nothing from selfishness or empty conceit, but with humility of mind let each of you regard one another as more important than himself; do not merely look out for your own personal interests, but also for the interests of others" (Phil. 2:3-4).

We are to be unselfishly submissive.

Submission, then, is a non-resistant attitude that counters selfishness of the flesh and is exemplified to us by God's Son, "who, although He existed in the form of God, did not regard equality with God a thing to be grasped" (Phil. 2:6).

God, in His wisdom, chose to institute a universal principle of order in the marriage relationship, so He ordained that "Christ is the head of every man, and the [husband] is the head of a [wife], and God is the head of Christ" (1 Cor. 11:3). This is accomplished when "wives [are] subject to [their] own husbands, as to the Lord" (Eph. 5:22). That is God's divine blueprint for the structuring of the marriage partnership. So true submission means a wife will acknowledge her place in God's order, voluntarily acquiesce to her husband's leadership, and trust that the Lord will use him as a directing factor in her life.

This principle applies whether or not the husband is saved. The husband is the head of his wife, period. Yet too many unequally yoked wives think that God is limited because their husbands are not Christians. If they are wise, they will use his God-given position to their advantage.

Susie learned that the hard way. She was quite distraught when she came to see me. She had inherited some property prior to her marriage and now had to decide whether or not to sell it. She was employed, so she used part of her income for upkeep and taxes. The property was becoming a financial burden to her, but the land had been in the family for generations and she hated to sell it.

She told me she had prayed and had asked a Christian attorney, Christian friends, and her Sunday school teacher what she should do, but had received conflicting counsel. "I simply don't know what to do," she confessed.

My first question was, "What does your husband think you should do?"

She looked surprised. "I don't know. I haven't shared the problem with him. He isn't a Christian and I wanted godly counsel, so I didn't ask his advice."

As we searched the Scriptures, she realized that God was not limited in the way He could use her husband. She immediately asked him what he thought she should do and was relieved when he took over the matter. He lifted the burden of the decision from her. He came up with a plan so that she not only kept her inheritance but turned it into income property.

Susie learned that she dare not shut out her husband from any facet of her life. The unequally yoked wife must respect her spouse's position as God's representative authority, trusting that He will work through her husband to accomplish His will in her life and marriage.

An unequally yoked wife can rest assured that God can and will use her unbelieving husband to direct her. He can formulate His desires through her mate. God is not limited because her husband doesn't believe.

The First-Peter-Three Principle

First Peter 3:1-4 tells what an unequally yoked wife must do so God can use her husband as a guiding element in her life, and so she, in turn, can be used by the Lord to draw her husband to Christ. God has given her a positive approach to the spiritual aspects of both her marriage and her own Christianity; the "how to's" of being a godly wife in such unique, and sometimes trying circumstances.

19

First, wives are told, "Be submissive to your own husbands so that even if any of them are disobedient to the word, they may be won without a word by the behavior of their wives" (1 Peter 3:1). Once again, the pages of God's Holy Word emphasize a proven truth: that actions speak louder than words. Her unbelieving husband will be won, not by what she says, but "as [he observes her] chaste and respectful behavior" (1 Peter 3:2). Since words come easily, but the sifting away of sinful behavior is a slow, tedious process, a wife would be apt to say one thing while being another. So the Lord imposed this restriction to protect Himself and the Christian wife from scorn and ridicule.

No one knows us better than our families. They're there when we lose our tempers, show our true feelings; when we let it all hang out. They know our weaknesses and our sin patterns. So if a Christian wife verbally shares her faith with her unbelieving husband and tells him what God's standards are and what changes he should make in his attitude and actions, she had better be ready to live up to those requirements herself. But because she still has that Old Sin Nature, because she is as human as the next person, she cannot. So, if she talks her faith, she can fail by example and disgrace both herself and the Lord.

To keep this from happening, God reverses the pattern. He instructs the unequally yoked wife to change her behavior, and as He transforms her into the image of Christ, her husband will *see* what God is like and her acted-out faith will convince him of the validity of her Christianity. But, while she is growing, if she backslides or blows her witness, her mate won't have grounds for judging, condemning, or harrassing her.

Actions Speak Louder Than Words

Next, Paul defines how the unequally yoked wife should act. She is to be chaste. That's a rather old-fashioned sounding word that means pure. Ruth shared what this means to her: that she must never let down on her standards or live in opposition to stated scriptural principles. "I always have to maintain the difference between Christianity and the world, and by example, show my husband how God's way is best.

"But," she cautioned, "being chaste does not mean being prudish or holier than thou. It means being godly, Spirit-filled."

It also means the unbelieving husband can trust his wife; that she will be loyal and devoted to him. She will be sexually monogamous and mentally faithful, not wishing he was other than who he is. (Most unsaved husbands are keenly aware that their wives wish they were Christians.)

It means her husband can expect his wife to speak favorably of him and hold him up in a complimentary light to her Christian friends. Chastity involves a total commitment to the marriage partner's welfare.

The unequally yoked wife also is to be respectful, to honor her husband's position and him as a person. I am sure that sometimes this is hard, especially if the husband is extremely worldly, but it is a command from the Lord. Several unequally yoked women told me that they cannot respect their husbands because they aren't saved. The wives are guilty of a sort of spiritual pride and tend to look down on their mates as less than worthy of respect because of this.

Others said they concentrate too much on their husbands' negative qualities, rather than their good ones (something all wives do at one time or another), and have to make a conscious effort to dwell on the positives which deserve respect.

The godly woman in Proverbs "does [her husband] good and not evil all the days of her life" (Prov. 31:12). Sometimes wives do irreparable damage to their husbands' reputations by the way they speak of them. I know there have been many instances when unequally yoked wives have portrayed, in their prayer requests, what deplorable people their husbands are. As others listen, they draw conclusions and often form wrong or unfair opinions. Respecting her husband means she will not downgrade him in the eyes of others, in any way.

It also means she will hold him in esteem personally. If a Christian woman cannot respect her unbelieving husband's words and worldly habits, at least she can honor him as her husband; as the man she married for better or worse. She can dignify the relationship about its circumstances by venerating his "office" in her life.

Too often unbelieving husbands are treated like second-class citizens. Diane confessed to me that she had been guilty of this attitude. She had what she called a "spiritual superiority" complex. She wasn't aware of it at the time, but she mentally put down her husband. She mocked his ideas and his reactions or responses and secretly made fun of his opinions.

Finally, one day, when she visited him at his office, she was struck by the tremendous respect his co-workers, his secretary, and his boss showed him. She shared how she got a knot in her stomach when she heard a man who is older and more experienced than her husband say, "Yes, sir," to him. And she was both frightened and ashamed when she saw how his young secretary looked up to and admired him.

"She came into the office with coffee for us and when John thanked her she didn't just say 'You're welcome.' She said, 'Is there anything else I can get for you? Anything you need?' "

Diane confided, "When I got to the car, I started crying. I was so ashamed. I hated myself. I thought about how sweet John is, and how handsome and appealing as a person. I spent the next three days praying and confessing my disrespectful attitude. John asked me if there was anything wrong and I told him I would talk with him about it when I was able to cope. He was so kind to me, without even knowing why I was hurting. And when I asked his forgiveness, he was upset that I was being too hard on myself.

"The thing that disturbed me most," she continued, "is that I was judging him not because of his actions or because he isn't a good husband, but because he wasn't what *I* wanted him to be. I was disrespectful to him because he isn't a Christian." Diane knows now that the best way a wife can show her unbelieving husband that God loves him is to treat him with esteem.

Emulating a Gentle, Quiet Spirit

Finally, the unequally yoked wife is to manifest the fruit of the Spirit. Rather than concentrating on outward beauty, she is told, "Let not your adornment be external only— braiding the hair, and wearing gold jewelry, and putting on dresses" (1 Peter 3:3). This doesn't mean she isn't supposed to dress nicely or make herself attractive, but that she should cultivate "the hidden person of the heart," concentrating on "the imperishable quality of a gentle and quiet spirit, which is precious in the sight of God" (1 Peter 3:4).

The meaning of "gentle and quiet spirit" is frequently misunderstood. The word *quiet*, as it is used in this passage, doesn't mean lack of noise or activity, but lack of agitation or harshness. It doesn't mean a godly woman is to be passive, complacent, or speak in a whisper. It doesn't mean she can't differ with her husband or that she has to be withdrawn or uncommunicative. It means she is to cultivate the peace of God in her life.

It won't be easy, but an unequally yoked wife is not supposed to worry about her husband's salvation. Instead, she has to leave him in God's hands, because if she doesn't, she'll try to convert him with words rather than actions. She mustn't be anxious about what is going to happen to him or their marriage. She is to concentrate on being the best wife she possibly can, loving and respecting her husband, enjoying their relationship, and leaving the results to God. When she does, she will not be "frightened by any fear" (1 Peter 3:6).

Longsuffering Sometimes Means Suffering Long

A majority of the unequally yoked wives said they wished there was some way they could warn their sisters in Christ, who are in similar situations, to be patient with the results of their husbands' unbelief. Sara wisely noted, "Sure, Tom swears sometimes and he doesn't see why I think it's so wrong to cheat on our income tax, but I lose my temper and get very judgmental. Those are sins, too, only I should know better because God sets my moral standards. Tom has to come up with his own."

She cautioned that unequally yoked wives need to be sure that what they are angry or impatient about is not their husbands' lack of spirituality. "I know sometimes I get bent out of shape about dirty socks in the middle of the floor or the fact that he didn't put out the trash, but inside my head I'm thinking, if only he was a Christian, things like this wouldn't happen. I camouflage my resentment by being impatient about other things."

These women stressed the danger of dwelling on the fact that a husband is not saved. They expressed the concern that when this happens, they automatically want to try to convert their mates by talking to them about the Lord, rather than by living the example. Denise feels that, "Many of us are negative instead of positive about our situations. We are defeated and act as if our husbands are a lost cause. Instead, we need to develop a gentle and quiet spirit by clinging to God's promises in hope! I know my negative attitudes come through as if I was wearing a sign. Ed can tell when I am down on him because he isn't Joe Christian."

Other practical suggestions these unequally yoked wives shared about implementing the First-Peter-Three principle are:

1. Remember, you take the Holy Spirit with you wherever you go. Don't avoid social functions that are important

to an unbelieving husband, and perhaps to his career, just because you are a Christian.

2. Be more relaxed and less condemning. Roll with the punches instead of making too much out of too little too often.

3. Work as hard at improving yourself and becoming the woman your husband wants you to be as you want him to work at improving himself and becoming the man you want him to be.

4. If you married in direct disobedience, admit your sin, confess it, then get on with your life. Christ died for that sin on the cross and piling guilt on yourself will only make you more critical of your husband's unbelief. You'll want him to come to the Lord to undo your mistake.

5. Have a Christian confidant—someone you can trust—to dump on when the going gets rough. Complain to and pray with her rather than nagging your husband or announcing his faults to your entire Bible study in the form of a prayer request. (That's disrespectful!)

6. Maintain a close relationship with the Lord. Study, read the Bible, pray, and obey. Concentrate on Christ; He's the only One who is perfect, anyway.

The apostle Paul noted that, "The woman is the glory of man" (1 Cor. 11:7). Solomon said, "He who finds a [true] wife finds a good thing, and obtains favor of the Lord" (Prov. 18:22 Amplified). A First-Peter-Three wife is a *true* wife: a favor from the Lord to her unsaved husband, a "good thing" who brings him pleasure and happiness. Ultimately, she can provide that necessary "God-element" that may change his life for eternity.

3

Hurts, Heartaches, and Hindrances

As we have seen, God has set forth many practical scriptural guidelines for marriage. Following them will greatly enhance the relationship, but it will not eliminate problems. It's one thing to study a beautiful blueprint and quite another to build a happy marriage.

No marriage is perfect. Hurts of all kinds do occur, especially in unequally yoked marriages. Christian women who are married to unbelievers face heartaches and hindrances in their marriages that Christian women who are married to Christian men normally don't.

Yet, a large majority of them eventually adjust to and overcome their difficulties. They are able to develop fulfilling marital relationships. They do this by admitting their problems and facing the reality of their situations. They have chosen to hold their heads high and let their human spirits be energized by the Holy Spirit. They are overcomers.

I asked the women I interviewed to share the greatest difficulties they encounter and practical ways they handle them. Each one, in some way, encouraged me to tell the readers of this book that happiness is possible in an unequally yoked situation, even if the marriage was in direct disobedience to God's command not to be unequally yoked. They stressed His grace and mercy and that it is possible to "do all things through Christ which strengtheneth me" (Phil. 4:13 KJV).

But I'm Married to an Unbeliever!

The first thing they had to learn was how to overcome their guilt about being married to an unbeliever. Flo noted, "I realized that God disciplines us for all ongoing sin that should be forsaken. My marriage is not a sin, even though I married Tim when I was a Christian and he was not. I am not supposed to forsake it just because he isn't a believer. I love my husband and want to stay with him. That is not a sin. That's God's desire for my life."

Most women who married in deliberate disobedience are aware of, but do not resent, the Lord's discipline. Basically, they reap what they sow. Wanda has a marvelous perspective. "God allows the consequences of direct disobedience or ignorance," she says, "when knowledge was possible, to develop a strong faith and godly character in the Christian wife. Perhaps that is the only way He can infiltrate our selfish nature and win an unbelieving husband."

Some women are convinced that the unrelenting burden they feel for their husbands is a form of discipline. Joyce said she hurts continually because, "Don doesn't have the same desire for Christ as I have and he has no religious convictions. Seeing him stumble through life without the Lord is hard."

Sara's grief is that, "More than anything I want Brent to *feel* loved by God. He can't, and that breaks my heart." Barbara voiced the sentiments of all unequally yoked wives when she observed, "My marriage is not bad or difficult, but it lacks the God-factor all Christians so badly need."

Polly, a Christian widow who married a man thinking he was also saved and found out later he was not, believes that for several years she punished herself when she discovered Martin wasn't a Christian. "As we all do, I married with good intentions. I didn't want to be alone. I wanted my young daughters to have a father. Then when I realized

27

Martin wasn't a Christian, I was totally devastated. I think I punished myself. My problems and struggles were of my own making because I was appropriating God's discipline, which I felt I deserved, instead of His grace."

Jan, who became a Christian after she married George, said she had never felt guilty because, "I was not spiritually accountable at the time. I didn't know God's will so I couldn't go against it. And, I've been forgiven. Christ nailed my sins to the Cross."

Regardless of how an unequal yoking occurred, a Christian wife must remember that, "there is therefore now no condemnation for those who are in Christ Jesus" (Rom. 8:1). She doesn't need to do penance for a sin that Christ erased on Calvary.

What if he Goes to Hell?

Almost all unequally yoked wives agree that the greatest heartache, and perhaps discipline, any one of them faces is the agony of knowing that when her unsaved husband dies he will pass into a Christless eternity and she will never see him again. Molly said, "It worries me so much because I know what hell is like and what Phil would go through if he dies without the Lord. None of us want to see our loved ones suffer, especially in the eternal pit of hell. That reality is a nightmare for me."

The only way for a Christian wife to cope with it is to put it into perspective in the light of the Word. She has to realize that rejecting Christ is her husband's choice. It isn't hers, because she has been told not to verbally witness to him. It isn't the Lord's, because it is His will that all come to repentance. God does not condemn anyone to eternal damnation. "God did not send the Son into the world to judge the world; but that the world should be saved through Him" (John 3:17). Rather, He provides the only way out—Jesus Christ.

Cecelia told me that the day she accepted the fact that her husband's salvation was dependent on him, and that God would never send him to hell because of anything she'd done, or to punish her for marrying him, she felt as if a huge weight had been lifted from her soul. "I have to leave him in God's hands and be the wife I'm supposed to be. I can't play the Holy Spirit, and I know Jack will have abundant opportunity to repent because God is just. God doesn't want him to go to hell, either."

On the other hand, the unequally yoked wife cannot live her life just waiting for her husband to receive Christ. She has to accept the fact that he could die unsaved. "I hope and believe," Cindy said, "but intellectually I know that everyone doesn't come to the Lord. That's a truth I have to face."

Neither should the Christian wife dwell on her husband's unbelief. If she thinks about it too much or too often, it will warp their entire marriage relationship.

"Sometimes when Mike and I have a real spiritual conflict, I get consumed by the fact that he isn't saved. It's almost as if he has horns, wears a red suit, and blows smoke. I see him as wicked and wayward," Karen admitted. "If I don't control it, it gets to the point where I think about it every time we have any sort of disagreement or he displeases me in any way."

Some unequally yoked wives admitted they want their husbands to become Christians as much for their own convenience as for their husbands' welfare. "I just get so tired of living with his worldliness and his carnal attitudes that I feel like crying out to the Lord to save me from him by saving him," Shirley confessed.

She suggested any time a wife starts concentrating on her husband's spiritual inadequacies that she pray out loud, and spiel her frustrations to the Lord until she has them off her chest. "God would rather I yell at Him about my anger and pain than yell at Paul."

Can he be a Good Father?

Probably the most intense, overt problem the Christian wife faces in her unequally yoked marriage is conflict over raising the children. They see the difference in lifestyles between their parents and may decide to follow the ways of the world rather than the way of the Lord. The believing wife has to find some way to counter this and to expose her husband's sin to their children without putting him down or undermining his position as their father. Children learn so much by observing that it puts a heavy load on the Christian mother to set a constant example of godly behavior, and at the same time not be overly critical of her husband.

Also, "There is an inclination to use the children to evangelize your husband," Karla mused. "I can't get away with asking him to pray with me when we go to bed or cuddling up in his lap and asking him to read me a Bible story at bedtime, but Danny and Danielle can, and sometimes I put them up to it. That's not right. It should be spontaneous on their part."

The unequally yoked wife has to be as willing to let God handle the salvation of her children, as she is to let Him handle it with her husband. She does have an advantage as a mother, however, because she can play an active part in their spiritual upbringing, whereas her role as a wife, in the spiritual sense, must be passive. But many times the unbelieving husband fears that his wife is instilling her faith in the children to turn them against him. So she must be sensitive about when and how she trains them, and she must do it not in a way that demeans their father, but in a way that edifies and glorifies the Lord.

Feeling Alone and Isolated

Another major hindrance in an unequal marriage is that the believing wife has no human spiritual head in her home. While it is true that God can and will use her husband to direct her—this is accomplished through God's sovereign control of circumstances and His literally superseding her mate's sin—in a Christian marriage it is done internally, through the indwelling presence of the Holy Spirit. So, although the Lord uses an unbelieving husband in practical ways, there is still a lack of spiritual communication between husband and wife.

Terri disclosed that "The thing that disappoints me most about my marriage is that I can't share anything spiritual with the person I love most. O sure, I tell him how God answers prayer and share what the Lord is doing, but he just doesn't understand. He believes in coincidence, not in answered prayer. I long for the day when he will be able to rejoice with me over the great things God is doing in our lives."

Spiritually, the unequally yoked wife is more or less on her own. Of course, she has the Holy Spirit, but in the reality of everyday living she has to decide herself if something is right or wrong in the eyes of the Lord. She doesn't have a husband to help her interpret her theology. She can listen to sermons, go to Bible studies, and develop Christian principles for living. But her husband may harass her for living according to God's standards, whereas a Christian husband will supplement a godly lifestyle.

No matter how many friends an unequally yoked wife has in her church, or how well received she is by the congregation, she still suffers from spiritual isolation. She has to go to church alone. Even if her husband does attend with her intermittently, she knows he is not there as an act of worship, or to fellowship with the Lord, but as a courtesy to her.

Compensation seems to be the solution to this dilemma. The unequally yoked wife must rely on the Lord for her spiritual guidance, rather than on her husband. She has to realistically face the fact that it is an impossibility for her husband to understand her spiritual needs, because he is not spiritually apprised.

Women in that situation advise that it helps to have a

woman friend as a spiritual substitute for her husband. This should be someone who will be a prayer partner, who will sit with her in church, who will interpret the Scriptures with her, and who will give advice on spiritual matters. Sometimes the "friend" can be a Christian couple, so the unequally yoked wife will get input from a male perspective. But she must never build a separate friendship with a man. Unbelieving husbands don't understand about brothers in Christ, and an unequally yoked wife is emotionally vulnerable to Christian men.

These women who have "been there" further advise that an unequally yoked wife should concentrate on doing husband/wife things with her husband, apart from church, rather than resenting the fact that she can't be involved in church-related couples' activities. Adele verified the value of such an approach. "Recently a lot of families from our church went to a Christian camp for the weekend. I wanted us to go so badly that I got in a sulky mood and Irv never knew why.

"One afternoon, when I was crying and praying, telling the Lord how much I wished our family could go, He said, why don't you have your own family camp? I got so excited I could hardly stand it!"

By the time Irv got home, Adele had planned a family outing. He was elated at the idea. So they took the kids and camped on the beach for two nights and had a great time together. "I felt so close to the Lord, listening to the surf, meditating on His Word as I lay on the sand in the sun. And Irv mentioned several times how touched he was that I had suggested doing it. We had a wonderful family camp!"

Compensation. God can meet our needs wherever we are, in any circumstances.

Do You Expect too Little?

As we have seen, there are many ways a husband's unbelief can affect the overall tenor of the marriage. One is that in the general contest of the relationship, a wife may not expect as much joy, pleasure, or satisfaction from her marriage as she would if her husband was a believer. Many admitted they believed their marriages could never be as fulfilling as Christian ones are. "His unbelief takes the edge off our pleasure and the good things that happen because underlying it all is the fact that he doesn't belong to the Lord," Laura explained.

Such an attitude can be disastrous because it's a fact of life that most people live up to what we expect from them. So if a wife expects her husband to be responsive and loving, and to develop his capabilities and reach his potential, she will affect his performance positively. Conversely, if she sees him as inadequate and lacking something she possesses, and if she expects him to be remote or critical, chances are he will oblige.

Yvonne commented that when she first came to Christ, she was shocked at how her respect for Randy diminished. "It wasn't long until I realized I was suffering from a case of spiritual superiority. *I* had God and *he* didn't. And I had been acting as if I was better than him. That made him feel hurt and rejected. He stopped being the kind of husband he'd been before my conversion. He stayed away from me, didn't talk to me or kiss me as much. I didn't see it then, but I was driving him away.

"Finally," Yvonne continued, "one night when we were in bed I took him in my arms and told him I knew I had been a brat; that I had been acting like a snob and that the truth of the matter was that I loved him even more since I'd accepted Christ."

She asked me to caution all unequally yoked wives about lowering their expectations to accommodate their husbands' unbelief. "Many unsaved husbands love their wives, are good providers, tender lovers, competent fathers, and generally nice guys. They deserve to be accepted on their own merits, not because of their spirituality."

33

Some *One* Has Come Between Us

Because the Christian's relationship with Christ is so precious and personal, it is easy for an unbelieving husband to become jealous of the Lord. Since this seems to be a widespread reaction, the unequally yoked wife must be extremely careful not to do anything that will make her husband feel he is in competition with God for her affections. Perhaps that is another reason why she is instructed to win him without a word. Verbalizing her intense feelings about God would only threaten her husband.

"Listen," Bob explained, "no man likes to feel he's second to anyone with his wife, and that includes second to God. Paula sure wouldn't like it if I spent as much time thinking about another woman as she does about Jesus."

Because the unsaved husband does not understand *who* Christ is, he cannot understand his wife's commitment to Him, and he may deeply resent the time she devotes to the Lord. Women who have faced this problem offered several suggestions to help alleviate it.

First, the wife must admit that her husband is probably jealous of the Lord, even if he doesn't know it. Second, she should not neglect her husband's needs, in any way, even for church or involvement in her personal ministry. Third, she must never make her husband feel she is choosing the Lord over him. She should not cut down on the quality or amount of time she spends with him to be involved in Christian activities.

Fourth, she must remember that it is Christ, and not the church, who demands her allegiance. She shouldn't confuse time spent with God with time spent at the church. Fifth, she should do Christian things—such as reading and studying the Bible, fellowshiping with other Christians, and instructing her children in the ways of the Lord—when her husband isn't around.

If Only . . .

Another problem, which was mentioned in an earlier chapter, is that many unequally yoked wives idealize Christian marriages and dream about what their marriages would be like "if only he was a Christian." This causes friction and may make a wife resent her husband because he isn't a believer. Bea confessed, "When I fantasize about what our marriage would be like if Larry was a Christian, I feel I have to forgive him for not being one, but that's God's job and not mine."

In some ways, our churches compound this difficulty. Some unequally yoked women are embarrassed by the fact that their husbands aren't Christians. "I try not to tell anyone because when I do they always act like, oh, you poor thing. Or, they assume I deserve anything that happens because I was disobedient, which I wans't, and married against the Lord's command about being unequally yoked. Then I get mad at Tony because he's put me in such a position by rejecting Christ."

Very few unequally yoked wives believe they are treated negatively by the Christian community, but they feel left out because so many church events center around husbands and wives. Melinda noted that, "I'm always made aware of *Christian* marriage relationships, in classes, in sermons, in the books I read and the lives I see, and it points up my own lack."

These women need to understand that if Christian marriages were so glowingly wonderful, there wouldn't be so many lessons taught, sermons preached, or books written on how to have a happy one. Christianity is not a panacea for all of our problems; it is a faith relationship with a God who is able to help us overcome sin.

How Can we Agree?

God also can control an unbelieving husband during the decision-making process. God can affect what he thinks and

35

does. An unequally yoked wife must not push or manipulate to get her way because she thinks it is God's way. If she does, rather than being a sounding board for her husband, she will become his conscience and block vital lines of communication. She will become his judge and jury. Instead of being available to listen to his problems and his ideas, she will pressure him, any number of ways, to get him to do what *she* thinks God wants done.

That is what Sarai did to Abram. God had appeared to him and promised that he would have multitudes of descendants, even though at the time he was almost ninety years old and they had no children. Sarai knew what the Lord had promised, but she got very impatient. Her human sensibilities wouldn't accept that she could become a mother, since she was far past childbearing age. She talked Abram into committing adultery with her handmaid, Hagar, so she would have a child for them.

Instead of waiting on the Lord, she blamed Him for her barrenness. "Sarai said to Abram, 'Now behold, the Lord has prevented me from bearing children. Please go in to my maid; perhaps I shall obtain children through her.' And Abram listened to the voice of Sarai" (Gen. 16:2).

Abram listened to the voice of Sarai! Never doubt the influence a wife has over her husband. She can use it either for God's glory or for her own personal gratification.

Well, Hagar conceived and Sarai was so jealous that she couldn't stand the sight of her maid. Sarai blamed Abram for what had happened. ("May the LORD judge between you and me"—Gen. 16:5.) So, in keeping with his wife's further wishes, Abram sent Hagar and her child into the wilderness. They would have died there if God had not supernaturally intervened.

Abraham listened to his wife, and even today we are paying for the sinful counsel she gave him, because the Lord founded the Arab nations through Abram's and Hagar's son, Ishmael. "He will be a wild donkey of a man, his hand will

36

be against everyone, and everyone's hand will be against him; and he will live to the east of all his brothers" (Gen. 16:12).

That conflict with the Arab countries still exists. It never would have happened if Sarai had not wrongly influenced her husband.

Although the unequally yoked wife is to be a helpmeet and counselor to her husband, she must influence him primarily through her prayers and her behavior. And, she must not assume that because she is a Christian, she automatically has a grasp on God's will.

The wife's role, then, is not to pressure her husband into doing things her way, but to trust God to lead him, through circumstances and external direction from the Holy Spirit. Jennifer has learned the secret of making such Spirit-controlled decisions. "Even if Gary isn't a believer," she observed, "I am. I have the Holy Spirit, so I can rely on the Lord to give us both the right answer, or to show me when to stand my ground or to back down, and to give me peace about giving in to my husband."

Here are some recommendations from unequally yoked wives who have mastered this technique. They warned that when God's will is presented to a woman through her unbelieving spouse, she may reject it unless she has let the Lord sensitize her heart to receive His message, regardless of who the messenger is. So first she should pray and ask the Lord to reveal His will to her.

Next, she needs to present her case based on facts, not on some ethereal spiritual reason. She should verbally communicate her reasons for feeling and thinking as she does. "The Lord told me" is insufficient proof for an unbelieving husband.

Also, she should state any objections she has to her husband's opposing view, but she must not attack him. She does not have to surrender what she believes is right, but she has to be willing to compromise, to reason with her husband, and to brainstorm for alternatives. Remember, that is God's suggested method in the decision-making process. "Come now, and let us reason together, says the LORD" (Isa. 1:18).

Attitude is important. She must abide by whatever rules of Christian conduct apply to the situation. She can disagree, but she mustn't be disagreeable. She can reason with her husband, but not be unreasonable.

Finally, if a mutual decision cannot be reached and her husband isn't willing to wait or talk further, she will have to let him make the final choice. Then she must abide by it graciously. Sandy told me how, when Ken needed a new car, she really pushed him to get a station wagon. "The kids are getting older and I had visions of piling swarms of whooping big teen-age boys into my two-door sedan. But Ken was adamant. He wanted a sporty car, although he conceded to getting one with a back seat so he could carry four passengers."

"I was furious," she continued. "Until the fuel crunch. He gets great mileage and next year I'm going to get a compact wagon that also gets good mileage. If we'd have bought a big wagon, we'd be stuck with an unsaleable gas guzzler." She sees now that Ken's decision was best for their family finances. Even though his motives for wanting a smaller car may have been selfish, God bypassed those to accomplish His will in the matter.

Who's in Charge?

There are four major areas where an unequally yoked wife must be careful not to inadvertently impose "God's" will on her husband. We have already discussed one; that of *making decisions*. She has to avoid the temptation to always have the final say, certain she knows what is best because she is a Christian.

The second area is *initiative*, where the wife, in order to control her husband's friends and social activities, becomes the instigator of all family plans. In many marriages, by nature, it seems the woman is the one who plans the dinner parties, evenings out, and backyard barbeques. But an unequally yoked wife may exclude her husband and bypass his wishes in order to create a more Christian atmosphere. She should include her husband when making plans and never accept or decline invitations without first consulting him. That is common courtesy.

The third area where role reversal sometimes occurs is *discipline*. Once a Christian woman starts using biblical standards for raising children, she may devalue her unsaved husband's input. She needs to learn how to incorporate godly principles into her and her husband's ongoing philosophy of parenting, which in many cases was established long before she came to Christ.

Marlene told how, before she accepted the Lord, when she and Harlan would be having a drink, sometimes they would give a sip to the kids. "As I grew in the Lord, I saw that wasn't right, so decided we shouldn't do it any more. I didn't tell Harlan how I felt, but the next time he did it, I hit the ceiling. I yelled at him that he was leading them astray and that he was breaking the law by giving liquor to minors."

Naturally, her husband was completely dumbfounded. She shared that after she had cooled off, she thought it through and apologized to him. "I told him the truth; that before I knew the Lord those kinds of things didn't matter, but now they do and that I feel as a Christian mother I have to protect my children from the dangers of alcohol. I told him I felt that by giving them a sip of beer we were telling them it's okay to drink and that when they are teen-agers they'll remember that."

She was blessed when Harlan not only understood, but said that was something neither of them had thought of before and it was a good point.

The unequally yoked wife must not try to be both a

Christian mother and father to her children, but rather the best mother she can be. She should ask her husband how he thinks they should handle behavior problems and share new insights she gains from her study of the Word. They should plan together, as a couple, their strategy for disciplining the children.

Children are quite perceptive, especially when it comes to knowing what is going on between their parents. They will recognize, perhaps before their parents do, that there is an underlying friction. They will play one parent against the other, to get their own way. Consulting on minor matters eliminates that kind of manipulation and makes it easier to communicate about major ones. When an unequally yoked wife includes her husband in this way, she is showing him that she respects his opinion and position.

The fourth area where role reversal predominates is *finances*; where the Christian wife tries to "control" the money so she can give to the church or buy Christian tapes and books. Scripture does not state whether a husband or wife should handle the family finances, but it does clearly show that the man is to be the basic provider and that their life together is a partnership. So the issue here isn't who should keep the books, maintain the budget, or write the checks, but the fact that finances are a joint responsibility. If a wife tries to control the cash flow so she can give to the Lord, then she does not have a clear understanding of what He expects from her.

Jodi did just what we are talking about. Instead of asking John if she could give some money to the church each week, she started smuggling it out of her grocery fund. Whenever she cashed a check she would write it for a few dollars over, then put that in the offering.

You can imagine how startled she was when John unexpectedly asked her, "Don't they ever take an offering at your church?" She said her face flushed and she stammered an affirmative answer.

"Well," he asked, "don't you think if you are going to go there, you ought to contribute something?"

She was so ashamed that she broke down and confessed what she'd done. She told John that another woman she knew, whose husband didn't believe as she did, wouldn't let her give to the church. And in some instances, that's true. But that doesn't mean a wife should sneak money from the family budget. God knows why she is not contributing financially, if her husband won't let her give. He does not want her to resort to sinful methods so she can give. Often an open, honest request to work some kind of donation into their financial picture will bring a positive response.

Obviously, there are many ways an unequally yoked wife can minimize the hurts, heartaches, and hindrances in her marriage. She can concentrate on what God is doing in her and her husband's lives, instead of on the fact that he is not saved. She can respect his views about child-raising and treat him as an equal in parenting. She can keep her expectations within the realm of the possible when it comes to spiritual matters, but not lower them in an overall sense.

She can eliminate her husband's jealousy toward God by putting him first, in an earthly sense, and making their marriage a priority over even the church or Christian friends. She can refrain from idealizing Christian marriages and remember that most of the problems she faces are common to all marriages, and are not contingent on the fact that her husband is not a believer.

Finally, she can adapt her marriage standards and incorporate godly ones into an ongoing pattern that she and her husband believe are best for them, rather than trying to impose spiritual externals on him. As she does this, with God's help, the hurts, heartaches, and hindrances will subside.

4

Do's for Marital Happiness

I would like to introduce you to three women who are unequally yoked. Each of them has been married to an unbeliever for many years.

Shirley beams when she talks about her husband. She
recently told a group of women that she thinks she is the
luckiest woman alive to have married a wonderful man like
Andrew. She admires, respects, and obviously loves him.
They are happily married.

Elaine and David have been married for thirty-five years.
They have had ups and downs, but haven't we all? She had
some difficulties raising the children, but she was such a
good wife in all respects that her husband gave her a free
hand in the spiritual realm. Now they are enjoying retire-
ment—traveling together and savoring the companionship.
They have a good marriage, one that many of David's unbelieving friends envy. They are happily married.

Donna and Ray are both approaching fifty. Donna is
the only one in her family who knows the Lord; her husband
and three grown children are unbelievers. They are a close-
knit family and have fun together. She participates in her
husband's hobby, auto racing. Although she has had to miss
church many Sundays to travel around the state with him,
she has done it willingly. He is openly proud of her. They
are happily married.

What's the moral of these stories? *You can be happy
though unequally yoked,* without compromising your faith
or your dedication to Christ. In this chapter we will look at

some do's that these, and other women like them, have put into practice that have made their marriages happy, enjoyable, and fulfilling. Some review what has already been discussed, some are new.

Expect to be Happy

We all anticipate that when we marry it will be a pleasurable, rewarding experience. No one enters into a lifetime relationship expecting to be unhappy. So what happens in an unequally yoked partnership that makes so many wives unhappy? Could it be that they expect to be miserable, to have insurmountable problems, because their husbands are unsaved? It is a fact that we get out of life what we put into it and expect from it.

Charlotte M. Yonge said, "Happiness? That would mean more contented with my station in life, striving to derive all possible benefits from it, to BEAUTIFY rather than alter it."[1] The unequally yoked wife has to believe she can be happy and fulfilled in her marriage. Rather than being discontented because she is married to a man who is not a Christian, she must concentrate on cultivating and enjoying peace and happiness where God has placed her. Instead of trying to alter her status, she should seek to beautify and derive every possible benefit from her life as it is. She should plan to be happy, and she most likely will be.

Expect Him to be Unreasonable

The fact that a Christian is married to an unbeliever does not have to cause unhappiness in the marriage. But it will, unless the unequally yoked wife expects her unbelieving husband to be unreasonable about spiritual things. Conversely, he probably thinks she is unreasonable about earthly matters.

---

[1]Charlotte M. Yonge, "Goldust," *Something to Live By*, Dorothea S. Kapplin (Garden City: Doubleday, 1945).

To him, the Bible is no better guidebook for living than his favorite "how-to" or self-help book. He undoubtedly enjoys going to the movies more than he does going to church. Sin is not an issue to him, as it is to his wife. Her godliness is threatening, convicting, and confusing to him. He does not understand it.

I have found that we Christians have a tendency to impose our personal idea of spirituality on everyone else. Wives, in particular, think they have the right and ability to set the terms for what their husbands' spiritual responses should be. I remember what our pastor told me when George accepted Christ. He warned, "You must never forget that your husband's spiritual life is in the Lord's hands. He doesn't need you to interpret what God is telling him to do, but to support him in it and pray for him if he strays from it."

The same is true if the husband is unsaved. His spiritual life is in the Lord's hands. He does not need for his wife to "play" God for him, but to be a representative of God to him.

Most of us can think back to the time when we were unbelievers, or were so carnal that no one could tell the difference. We need to remember how offensive it was when anyone tried to approach us about the Lord.

I recall a time when I was so deeply involved in sin that I wasn't giving so much as a thought to the things of God. I was worried because my daughters were going to vacation Bible school at a church where they pushed Bible reading, talked too much about Jesus, and had altar calls. I didn't want my children to become fanatics.

During that same period of time, I received a letter from my cousin, telling me about the peace God had given her when her brother died. She quoted Scripture and rejoiced about their being together in eternity. I was so appalled that I actually made fun of the letter. I was so sinful that I was totally unresponsive to spiritual things; I was even repulsed by them.

The unbelieving husband probably feels that way. So

if his wife, who claims to love him and want what is best for him, tries to force spiritual issues, he will balk, at both her and God. She needs to maintain a low profile about the Lord and spiritual matters. She needs to understand when he is disinterested or even belligerant about church, Bible studies, and her relationship with the Lord. It is reasonable for him to be unreasonable about her lifestyle.

Expect Problems as a Part of Life

Remember, an unequally yoked wife may have a tendency to idealize Christian marriages and possibly blame many normal problems on the fact that her husband is unsaved. This is a false assumption and can cause irreparable damage to the relationship.

The truth is that many of the problems the unequally yoked wife faces in her marriage are common to all marriages and are not solely due to the fact that her husband is not a Christian. People are people. We all have strengths and weaknesses, faults and virtues. Some Christian husbands have tempers and are at times unreasonable and unappreciative and disobedient to the Lord. Christian couples argue, disagree, and act selfishly.

In a setting as intimate as marriage, where every facet of an individual's personality and character are shared, and in some ways are infringed upon by another, there will be conflict and, sometimes, disorder. The major difference between the Christian couple who has problems and an unequally yoked situation is that both believers are indwelt by the Holy Spirit. He is an inner controlling factor in the overall relationship.

Millie shared that she assumed that every problem she and Tom had in their marriage was due to the fact that he was not a Christian. No matter what difficulties they faced, she dismissed any personal responsibility because she was saved and he was not. So when he blew up at her for spending too much money, and it happened to be a time when she had given a generous amount to a missionary fund, she wrote it off as his not wanting her to donate to the church.

As time passed, Tom repeatedly told her she had to cut back on expenditures. He finally informed her that he was going to give her a household and personal allowance instead of leaving the checkbook with her, so he could control what she spent.

She was furious! She called him selfish. She was raving because he threw away money on golf fees and beer. She was convinced he was persecuting her for being a Christian. When we talked, I suggested that she list, in detail the purchases she had made in the past three months. She discovered that she was spending almost one-third of their net income on whatever she wished, without even consulting her husband.

"I know now that I purposely blamed Tom's unbelief so I would not have to face the fact that I am a spendthrift. I was causing our financial problems and didn't want to accept the responsibility for it." The unequally yoked wife has to be careful not to use "he's not a Christian" as a cop-out for her failings.

Look For Positives

Although every unbeliever is an unregenerated sinner, that does not mean that he is a reprobate. George and I have often talked about how the only noticeable change in his life, after he accepted the Lord, was his inclination toward spiritual things. Even before he became a Christian, George was a good man. He was gentle, kind, honest, dependable, and had a sense of humor. That's why I married him.

A Christian wife should look for positive character and personality assets in her unsaved husband. What qualities made her want to marry him in the first place? In what ways is he maturing and growing? What are some things he does that please her and make her happy?

When I teach, I sometimes ask the class to list five things they dislike about their husbands. When the lists are completed, I ask them what they think would happen in their marriages if they spent an hour a day dwelling on each negative they have recorded. After the laughter subsides, we conclude that if we spent time thinking about our husband's faults we could make ourselves miserable within a period of a few hours.

Next, I suggest that they look at every fault on the list, pray about it, and submit it to God. Then they should tear up the list and, through an act of their will, erase those things from their minds.

Finally, we make a list of positives about our husbands. Each woman plans to concentrate on and compliment her husband about at least one of those facets during the next week. When the women return to class, the ones who have worked toward this goal tell glowing stories about the warm, loving responses they are getting from their mates.

An unequally yoked wife must not get lost in negatives, especially the fact that her husband is not saved. She should look for, hope for, and expect the best.

Be Genuine

The world is inundated with phonies, hypocrites: men and women who say one thing and do another. Webster defines a hypocrite as someone who pretends to be better than he really is, or who pretends to be pious or virtuous without really being so.

In the twenty-third chapter of Matthew, the Lord delivers a scathing rebuke against religious hypocrites. He calls them fools, blind guides, whitewashed tombs, vipers, and serpents. Repeatedly, He addresses them as hypocrites. The Greek word for hypocrite means "actor." He indicts them for being phonies; for playacting at being godly.

The world responds much the way Christ did to religious hypocrisy. So will an unbelieving husband. Therefore, the unequally yoked wife must act out her Christianity in sincerity and with conviction. What she does, or does not do, will affect her husband's opinion of what he thinks a Christian should be.

For instance, is the wife judgmental? Even unbelievers know Christians are not supposed to judge others. Does she use earthy language? Is she unreasonably impatient with the children? And what about her relationships with the neighbors and her husband's friends? Is she super-critical, aloof, and pious, or does she minister to them with a servant's heart?

The apostle John observed that "the one who says he abides in Him ought himself to walk in the same manner as He walked" (1 John 2:6). An unbelieving husband has a right to expect his Christian wife to emulate Christ and to fault her if she does not.

Be Loyal

When Bathsheba gave her son, Solomon, advice on how to choose a wife, she placed faithfulness at the top of the list of admirable, wifely attributes. She counseled her son that an excellent wife (who, incidentally, is hard to find) is so dependable that "the heart of her husband [can trust] her, and he will have no lack of gain. She does him good and not evil all the days of her life" (Prov. 31:11-12).

We have already seen that this kind of faithfulness goes beyond mere physical fidelity, to the depths of the soul. A husband should be able to trust his wife with his *heart*: his emotions, his will, his awareness, his intellect—with his total being. And, a godly wife will always and forever look out for her husband's best interests.

An unequally yoked wife can do her husband immeasurable harm by advertising the fact of his unbelief. I am not saying she should keep it a secret, but she must keep it in perspective. Marriage is a covenant between two people and the Lord, even if one or both of them do not have a personal relationship with Him. In our society, when someone makes

48

a legal contract, he is expected to carry out its terms to the best of his ability.

The same is true in a marriage. God's stipulations are unconditional. A wife is to be loyal to her husband, unless there are extreme extenuating circumstances. Those must be dealt with as exceptions, not as the rule.

What does wifely loyalty involve? Basically, it means she sees, hears, and speaks no evil about the man to whom she is married. She puts *his* best foot forward in the way she talks about him and the way her attitudes portray their relationship. The things a wife implies or tells others about her mate reflects on her. "Be to his virtues very kind; be to his faults a little blind," is good advice.

Put God First

There is no doubt that the unequally yoked wife is in a precarious position. There will be times when she has to choose between her husband and her God. She must adhere to the principle that *in all things Christians are commanded to put God first.*

When Peter and the apostles were hauled before the council and threatened with imprisonment, they testified, "We must obey God rather than men" (Acts 5:29). The principle *all* believers are required to follow is that we are to put God and His law before any man or man-made law.

Although the concept is simple, acting it out is not. The unequally yoked wife cannot assume arbitrarily, in all situations, to know what God wants. So she has to evaluate each decision in the light of that standard. The best way to approach gray areas is to look at Christ's example. What did He do in similar predicaments? Is there a specific command in Scripture regarding the circumstances? Will what she is being asked to do strengthen or weaken her witness? And, most of all, will it please her husband without detracting from Christianity? Remember, there is a monumental difference between self-righteousness and the righteousness of God!

Rely on the Character of God

Ultimately, everything any Christian does must be viewed in the light of the character of God. No theology will work if it is not intrinsically related to the One who established it. Too often we are trapped by our own lack of faith into looking at our circumstances instead of at our Lord, who is Master of all things.

It is important that an unequally yoked wife understand how God's attributes relate to her protection and well-being. God is *sovereign*, so nothing can or will happen to her that He does not direct or permit. She is in His hands.

God is *immutable*. He never changes. If He was capable of delivering His saints in the past and saving them from their sin, He can still guide and protect an unequally yoked wife, no matter how intense or unhappy the situation.

God is *omnipresent*. He is always with her, even in the most heated or unpleasant times in the marriage. He will never leave her. He is *omnipotent*, so He can control even the most impossible of situations. He spoke and the world came into being. His power is complete, infinite, unlimited. He can act, speak, and invade enemy territory on her behalf and accomplish what He wishes, when He wants.

God is *perfect justice;* impartial and fair in all His dealings. He makes perfect decisions without bias. Therefore, anything He chooses to let happen to her will be fair and for her welfare.

God is *love*. Therefore, when she is rejected, hurt, and feeling unappreciated, she can turn to Him and He will compassionately respond to her needs. God is *merciful*. He does not give her what she deserves; He bestows lovingkindness, not condemnation. He also is *gracious*, so when her human resources break down, God is there to pour out His riches and blessing.

God is *faithful*. He is dependable and has set standards that never vary. He will keep every promise He has made.

He will never let her down. He will undergird and support her even if everything else collapses. He is her God and He is there.

God is *wise* and *omniscient*. He never misuses His position. He has total insight and perfect discernment. He knows things she will never know, including the end from the beginning, so He is better qualified to manage her life than she is. And, God is *patient*. That is why He overlooks her mate doing things that she finds intolerable. That is why, when she wishes God would knock her husband to his knees and make him pray to be saved, He endures, waits, and is serenely diligent. He uses restraint when He is provoked, because He is longsuffering.

Because God is *eternal*, time does not matter to Him as it does to us. When we want something, we want it yesterday. But God is so great, so vast, so unfathomable that He is not limited in any aspect of His being. Time does not engulf Him. Our selfish demands do not sway Him. His motive always is love.

Every unequally yoked wife can rest in the fact that her destiny, and that of her husband and family, is in the hands of an infinite, magnificent God and that she is not at the mercy of her circumstances. She can control her situation by trusting the Lord and by doing what He has commanded. She can be happy, even if she is unequally yoked.

5

Don'ts for Marital Happiness

In recent years we've heard a lot about the power of positive thinking, but there is also such a thing as the power of negative thinking. Just as there are ways we should act and think, there are also things we shouldn't think or do. In the first psalm, David noted that we will be happy if we refrain from certain behavior: "How blessed is the man who does *not* walk in the counsel of the wicked, *nor* stand in the path of sinner, *nor* sit in the seat of scoffers!" (Ps. 1:1).

All but two of the Ten Commandments, which are mankind's basic code of moral and religious conduct, are "do nots." You shall *not* have other gods before God, make idols or worship them, take the name of the Lord in vain, murder, commit adultery, steal, bear false witness, or covet.

This is how the power of negative thinking works: There are things a godly wife must not do, things which, when she abstains from doing them will, through their absence, bring blessing. In this chapter we will review and expand on some of those things, which a Christian wife should not do if she wants the Lord to bless her marriage.

Don't Put up Communication Barriers

As we noted when we examined 1 Peter 3, the unequally yoked wife is not supposed to "talk" her husband to Christ or use the Bible as a weapon to try to get him to change his evil ways, but neither should she put up communication barriers in other areas. Marriage is a partnership where the intellect and emotions must be shared, as well as bodies and abodes. Marriage is a relationship in which two people are free to divulge their views, concerns, feelings, and expectations.

Communication is an art; it has to be developed. Some of the best "how to" advice I ever got on the topic came from a sweet, Christian grandma who had been married to an unbeliever for forty-three years. She taught me what she called three ear openers: look, love, and listen.

She said that when you want to tell someone something, whether it's good news or bad, first you should *look* at him and see if he is ready to hear what you have to say. "Read" his eyes and facial expression; sense his mood. Take into account what he is doing right at that moment.

Next, whatever you say, say it with *love*. Love doesn't shout or nag; it corrects without condemning, and counsels without demanding its own way. Finally, you have to be willing to *listen* ("With your mouth tight shut," according to my surrogate grandmother) to whatever a person says back to you, whether you want to hear it or not. And remember, you can hear with your heart as well as your ears.

Beyond that wise philosophy, an unequally yoked wife will be better equipped to communicate with her husband if she understands that *conflict* is a basic part of the communication process. You may be familiar with Mrs. Billy Graham's famous observation that, in a marriage, if two people always agree, one of them is unnecessary.

Solomon, in his wisdom, noted that, "Iron sharpens iron, so one man sharpens another" (Prov. 27:17). We get hung up on conflict because we've been conditioned to believe that it is bad, even sinful. It is not. It is a tool God uses to help us mature. It's our reactions to conflict—anger, defensiveness, judgmentalism—that are the problem. So, if a Christian can understand what conflict is and how to handle it, she will be better prepared to cope with it in her marriage.

In Ephesians 4:29, God has outlines four standard for godly communication. His pattern is, "Let no unwholesome word proceed from your mouth, but only such as is good for edification, according to the need of the moment, that it may give grace to those who hear."

That short verse contains some basic qualifications for proper speech. One, whatever is said *must be wholesome:* pure and clean. Two, *it must edify the hearer,* not destroy his dignity, degrade him, or tear down his spirits. This doesn't mean it is wrong to criticize, but the criticism must be constructive, truthful, and spoken in love.

Three, the words that are spoken *must be appropriate.* Sometimes things need to be said, but not *when* we say them. Four, whatever is said *must give grace,* blessing, and pleasure to all who hear, even if what is being said was not meant for their ears.

The only communication limitation the Lord imposes is in the one area where an unbeliever lacks understanding, that of spiritual truth. Since an unsaved husband is not spiritually appraised, his Christian wife's knowledge in that sphere is to be communicated by her actions rather than through her words. This bond of silence will keep her from becoming proud over the fact that she grasps concepts which her husband cannot. It keeps her from becoming arrogant about her spirituality.

Don't Flaunt Your Spirituality

One of the most potent statements the Spirit directed the apostle Paul to make is: "Knowledge makes arrogant, but love edifies" (1 Cor. 8:1). And we Christians certainly are prone to be proud of what we know and to impose our superior interpretations of God's Word on everyone around us. An unequally yoked wife must be doubly cautious not to think of herself as better than her husband just because she knows Scripture and he does not. She may be more spiritually adept but she needs to use what she knows to build him up, not to put him down.

"I had a terrible time with this," Jenny said with a

54

laugh. "I believe the Bible gives us God's perspective about how we should live and any time Roger said something that disagreed with my interpretation of Scripture, I'd contradict him and tell him he was wrong. I measured everything he said and did by my supposedly superior standards.

"Finally," she continued, "one Saturday one of my friends came over for coffee and Rog sat and talked with us about the world situation. When he left she asked me what was the matter with me; what was making me treat Roger that way. I was shocked. I honestly didn't know what she meant. She told me I'd taken exception to everything he'd said. What it boiled down to was I thought his idea about what should be done in the Middle East was stupid because it didn't fit in with my views on endtimes prophecy."

Jenny said she spent the next few days listening to herself and was ashamed of what she heard. "Fortunately, Rog didn't know why I was on his case so he didn't blame the Lord for the way I was acting. When I realized what I was doing, that I had a bad pride problem, thinking I knew so much, I made sure it never happened again."

The unequally yoked wife has to remember that she and her husband are both sinners; the variation is that she is saved and he is not. But that doesn't make him any less of a person or less deserving of dignity and respect.

Don't be Dogmatic

One way she can squelch feelings of spiritual superiority is by avoiding dogmatism. When someone is convinced she is right, it's easy to be arbitrary. So, it is easy for a Christian wife, who knows God's truth, to become dogmatic about her beliefs.

Not too long ago I heard a pastor say that he is convinced that the only doctrine in Scripture on which all true believers agree is that we have to believe on the Lord Jesus Christ to be saved. A step beyond that, he noted, some think you receive Him silently, by making a commitment in your heart; others by being baptized in water; and some may say conversion happens when a person speaks in tongues. Still others believe it takes place only when someone makes a public confession of faith, and every group can back up their views with Scripture. His point was that dogmatism can be deadly if carried beyond basic convictions.

Sue Ellen shared that she had been dangerously dogmatic about where she and her husband should go to church. She constantly prayed for Rick's conversion and was elated when, with no prodding, he told her he wanted to go to church with her one Sunday. The sermon that day happened to be about tithing, and Rick saw it as a "hype for money." He told his wife how he felt and suggested that perhaps they could go somewhere else the following week.

Instead of being thrilled that he wanted to go to church again, despite what had been an unsatisfactory experience for him, Sue Ellen tried to defend the pastor, explaining that he seldom preached about money. "I remember telling him, besides, what he said was right and I love that church and all my friends go there. I wanted him to go to *my* church, so he could learn their doctrine. I begged him to go there with me just one more time, but he wouldn't. Would you believe *I* got mad at *him* for being stubborn?" she said, laughing.

Sue Ellen said that as she started praying, the Holy Spirit convicted her about her attitude and what she had said. "Looking back, I couldn't believe I had been so dogmatic. Here I'd been waiting for years for a break like that. Then I didn't recognize that God was answering my prayers, and leading us to a church of His choosing, when He dropped it in my lap."

She said that she knows she should have been so grateful that she would have gone to church anywhere, if Rick was willing to go too. "Somewhere in the back of my mind I'd always assumed that if he started going to church it would be where I was already a member. That was the way I wanted it, but God had other plans."

While such an assumption is understandably normal, it is not necessarily right. An unequally yoked wife must keep in mind that what matters spiritually is that her husband place his faith in Christ and acknowledge him as Savior, not that he go to her church or do it her way or interpret every doctrine as she does. She must be open-minded, rejecting prejudices and stereotypes, eliminating preconceived ideas that are based on habit and conjecture rather than fact.

If an unequally yoked wife is open-minded, rather than legalistic, she will be more approachable and less threatening to her husband. She doesn't have to compromise her beliefs but she should be willing to respect, allow for, and examine those which differ from hers, even if she knows they are incorrect.

Don't Second-guess God

If an unequally yoked wife is open-minded, she will not nurture preconceived ideas about how or when the Lord will bring her unsaved husband into the fold. She should not try to second-guess God's plan or timing in her husband's salvational process. There is no way she can know when, how, or if he will come to Christ, so if she anticipates what God, or her husband, is going to do, she will be frustrated and disappointed.

Monica was certain if she could just get Jeff to listen to a certain tape, read a specific Christian book, or go to some church function, he would accept Christ. So she was always manipulating to make that happen. She'd leave books lying around, open to the page she wanted him to read. She'd loudly play the tapes she decided he needed to hear, hoping he would listen to what was being said. And, she was always asking him to go to some church dinner or program with her.

It didn't work. He never looked at any of the books. The only portions of the tapes he ever seemed to hear were the parts with which he disagreed. And although he sometimes went to church functions with Monica, it was like any other social outing to him.

Consequently, Monica was always disappointed. She'd get depressed because Jeff didn't respond the way she wanted him to. Each time she suffered a letdown, she blamed her husband and eventually ended up angry at him because he didn't do what she thought he should. That would be an easy trap to fall into.

In 1 Corinthians, chapter 7, after Paul has given the marriage guidelines and confirmed that if an unbelieving mate chooses to leave, the Christian is freed from the relationship, he makes this statement: "For how do you know, O wife, whether you will save your husband?" (1 Cor. 7:16). He is pointing out that there is no way a Christian wife can know if God plans to use her as the instrument of her husband's salvation. Chances are, if He allows the unbeliever to leave, He is not. But, she *cannot* know! How could she? How can anyone? If she assumes she does know, then she will do what Monica did and try to usurp the role of the Holy Spirit. Or, if the marriage has deteriorated to the place that the unbeliever wants to leave, she will try to hang on to a relationship that should be terminated. A wife doesn't have to stay with an unsaved husband so she can save him.

Marion shared her perspective. She was married to Frank for thirty-seven years. He never accepted Christ. "Knowing he would go to hell when he died bothered me a great deal. At first I tried to discuss God's Word with him many times, until he simply said he didn't believe as I did and never would. Since I wasn't able to alter his opinion, I did what I was sure God wanted me to do. I tried to be patient and live a good Christian example. I loved and cared and prayed he would change and believe Jesus was the way, the truth, and the light.

"That never happened," she continued. "For thirty-seven years I longed and prayed that Frank might become a believer. I wanted it for him; I wanted it for myself; I wanted

58

it for us. But after he told me he would never believe as I do, I just knew I had to leave him in God's hands. I did all I could. The Lord did all He could, but Frank never accepted Christ."

Marion says she is glad that she didn't live her life anticipating her husband's conversion. "I just tried to have a congenial relationship with him in other areas and enjoy every day for what it was, so I have a lot of good memories. I concentrate on those and try not to think about the fact that Frank is in hell. But when I do, the Lord reminds me he's there as a result of his sin, not mine."

Marion has peace because she accepted God's will for her husband's role in their marriage, even though she didn't know what would happen concerning his salvation. She didn't try to force her spirituality on him or dictate what God should do. An unequally yoked wife must be careful not to make assumptions about what, when, how, or if the Lord will do something in her husband's life. She must never presume on God by thinking she can determine or control how or when her husband will become a Christian.

Don't Expect Mercy Without Justice

Finally, a Christian woman cannot expect God to honor her disobedience if she willfully married an unbeliever. She should expect to be disciplined and accept it as part of her growth. She must realize that the Lord isn't disciplining her to get back at her for marrying out of His will, but to lead her into future obedience.

She may not like what happens, but she should keep it in perspective: "All discipline for the moment seems not to be joyful, but sorrowful." It may not be pleasant, but it serves a purpose: "Yet to those who have been trained by it, afterwards it yields the peaceful fruit of righteousness" (Heb. 12:11). God's discipline is training in righteousness; it is how

He teaches His children to become spiritual adults. And it doesn't last forever. There is an afterwards.

The key to enduring God's discipline is acceptance. "Do not reject the discipline of the LORD, or loathe His reproof" (Prov. 3:11). Rather than making excuses and balking at what the Lord is doing in her life, if an unequally yoked wife will openly receive what God has for her, she will better adapt to her marriage and her husband. She must believe He is doing it in love, "For whom the LORD loves He reproves, even as a father, the son in whom he delights" (Prov. 3:12).

Also, an unequally yoked wife must remember that God doesn't make her husband sin, or purposely make her life miserable because she disobeyed. Connie noted that, "Mostly, God's discipline has come packaged in my reaping what I sowed. I knew Kent drank before I married him. I knew he was extravagant. Now, I have to live with a party-boy who spends our money much too readily on the wrong things. That's not God's fault. But His discipline is that every time I balk or complain, He reminds me that's the price I'm paying for my self-indulgence.

"I am learning a lot from living with the consequences of my sin," she continued, "and so is Kent. The Lord uses His discipline to get our attention and point out problems, so we can work harder at building our marriage in a positive way." Connie has learned to accept and use God's discipline as a powerful, formative force in her life.

An unequally yoked wife will be more satisfied in her marriage and more accepting of her husband if she uses the power of negative thinking: if she *does not* build communication barriers, feel or act spiritually superior, be dogmatic, or try to second-guess the Lord's plans for her husband's life. She must learn to appreciate His loving discipline, live in the now, accept the relationship for what it is, and believe she can be happy when she refrains from doing things which will block God's blessing.